Open Heart

Open Heart

poems by

Nicole Farmer

© 2025 Nicole Farmer. All rights reserved.
This material may not be reproduced in any form, published,
reprinted, recorded, performed, broadcast,
rewritten, or redistributed without
the explicit permission of Nicole Farmer.
All such actions are strictly prohibited by law.

Cover design by Shay Culligan
Cover image by Geirom on Pexels
Author photo by Anna Caterina

ISBN: 978-1-63980-718-5

Kelsay Books
502 South 1040 East, A-119
American Fork, Utah 84003
Kelsaybooks.com

for my family, by birth and chosen

open—adj.   1. allowing access, passage or a view through an empty space

2. exposed to the air or to a view; not covered

3. available for business, officially admitting customers or visitors

4. frank and communicative; not given to deception or concealment

5. allowed to vibrate along its whole length (music)

6. not containing any of its limit points (mathematics)

heart—noun   1. a hollow muscular organ that pumps the blood through a circulatory system by rhythmic contraction and dilation

2. the central or innermost part of something

verb   1. (informal) like very much; love

from the New Oxford American Dictionary

Acknowledgments

Thank you to the editors and readers of the following journals in which these poems were first published, sometimes in an earlier version:

Adelaide Literary Magazine: "the dancer," "Sunday Ironing"
Bacopa Literary Review: "car wash orgasmic whirl" (Best Prose Poem 2021)
Big Whoopie Deal: "How to Drive Your Car"
Burgeon Magazine: "Rain (sex) Rain (sex) Rain," "MJM & me"
Drunk Monkeys: "the dancer," "How to Walk Your Dog"
The Closed Eye Open: "MJM&me"
Great Smokies Review: "severed," "Yiva"
Inisfree Poetry Journal: "car conversation en route to the airport"
Kakalak: "Exalted"
The Mid-Atlantic Review: "Rain (sex) Rain (sex) Rain"
Pine Song: "Fall Turning" (Honorable mention, North Carolina Poetry Society, Laurette Prize)
Poetry South: "Betty Makes a Five-Layer Cake with a Blowtorch"
Poetry Breakfast: "my mother was a dancer"
The Raven's Perch: "Tree I Desire"
Sad Girls Club: "Crashy"
Suisun Review: "How to Walk Your Dog"
The Tulsa Review: "Purgatorio"
Wild Roof Journal: "What Is Lost What Is Blue," "vanish," "drift," "Wounded"
Wisconsin Review: "Sunday Ironing"

The poem "Saved" appeared in HONEST SONNETS by Nicole Farmer, published by Kelsay Books, July 2023. "Fall Turning" was shortlisted for the 2024 Kelsay Books Women's Poetry Contest.

*****

Many thanks to the supportive writing community I have found through various classes and workshops in North Carolina. I wish to thank: Kathleen Calby, my first reader and trusted editor, Cindy Appleby, and Josephine Spilka for their friendship and advice. Warm hugs to Susan Steadman, my role model and fellow wordsmith, and my soulmate, Karen Clarke, for her enthusiasm. This collection wouldn't have come to fruition without the wisdom and guidance of my esteemed teachers through the Great Smokies Writing Program: Scott Branson, Kenneth Chamlee, Richard Chess, Brit Washburn, and Whitney Waters. Thank you to Jose Hernandez Diaz who taught me so much about prose poetry and absurdism. As always, my love and thanks go to my husband, Mark, and my sister, Carrie, for their patience and encouragement.

Contents

Purgatorio	15
severed	16
What Is Lost, What Is Blue	18
Tree I Desire	19
drift	21
Betty Makes a Five Layer Cake with a Blowtorch	22
How Do We	23
Rain (sex) Rain (sex) Rain	24
the dancer	25
MJM&me	26
Funeral Day	27
How to Walk Your Dog	28
Sunday Ironing	29
car wash orgasmic whirl	30
Ylva	31
my mother was a dancer	32
How to Drive Your Car	34
Saved	35
car conversation en route to the airport	36
late summer	37
vanish	38
Crashy	39
Listening	40
Fall Turning	42
Wounded	43
Exalted	44
empty	45
Open Heart	46

"To love another person is to
see the face of God."

—Victor Hugo

Purgatorio

after Amanda Moore

I know nothing of knitting
but what I can braid together from
this yarn of yearning
& fashion some sort of hairshirt
to cover my broken chest.

The mountains surround my home
& my fitful dream bed where
my mind struggles to fix this fissure nightly.

Trucks race by my window.
Headlights transform blinds into bars on my walls.

The moon is a bright O of seduction.
She mesmerizes my sleepless hours.

Mysteries of my daughter bubble in my brain
like a cauldron of misunderstanding
an unravelling spool of heartstrings
& I miss her
& I miss her more.

I am the stranger.
My penance = waiting.

severed

in every family—pain
in every life—a door unhinged

how much time will it take
to forget
how you left me
just three days before mother's day
when you told me:
we are thinking of having children
but I could never trust
you with them
would have to protect them
from you (echo in my head: *from you from you from you*)

and half my body goes numb with the shock   (clang)
of being
S
L
I
C
E
Down the middle   (thud)

one half of my body falls to the ground like a felled tree

no breath will come/no words/as my left hand holds
the phone/and I listen to the swish of
your sword being wiped and sheathed/all the way
from LA LA Land/where you stand in
some unknown room/I have never seen/

in total whiteness   (void)
or maybe in front of a Hollywood
green screen
hard-faced in your shining armor while
I gaze out with my

one remaining eye   (numb)
at the late
spring evening breeze
blowing the silver grass
to green/and back to silver/again

What Is Lost, What Is Blue

after Noor Hindi

I am remembering your eyes. I am gathering joy. *Mi hija.* I rush to Lowes to pilage their paint samples. I scan the choices and search my memory for your exact eye color. Nothing compares. It has only been since Christmas, still I can't image your sparkling orbs in the California sun. *Ma fille.* Crystal Lake. Jamaican Dream. Sea Wind. Dolphin Blue. When I say blue I mean pain. Estrangement. *Mia miglia.* When I say blue I mean you have sent me to the moon. I strain to see your aqua world through the tiny spaceship window, but you have stolen one of my eyes. Blue Echo. Sapphire. Below Zero. Ice Cave. You freeze me out, but my heart still waits for you. *Betee.* I struggle to crawl inside your cerulean cave but you have erected bloody word spears in my path. When did I lose you? *Nae Ttal.* Those frigid teen years? Big Chill. Valley of Glaciers. Blue Flame. Burn me as you like but when my charred skin peels I will still be standing here, raw, with love in reserve. *Meine Tochter.* Midsummers Dream. Symphony of Blue. Gentle Sea. There in your Hollywood home you can wander to the Pacific shore any day you like. I can swim the continent to arrive waterlogged and you will scrub salt and sand in my wounds. *Doch.* Certainly, we have done this before. Cycles of trauma and triumph. You play your part, I'll play mine. Pain in our veins for generations. *Watashi no musume.* Open your heart. When I say blue I mean hope. *Abnati.* Forgive me, Blue.

Tree I Desire

Dawn tree, dripping tree, tree of stillness
and wind whispered tree dancing in the dusk.
Tree of satin red heart leaves.
Moon tree, tree of tomorrow, tree of rain.
Tree in my hair, tree in my veins, tree of my eye.
Honeybush vanilla caramel tree of thee I sing.
Tree I run to for comfort.
Dead tree split open wide as a sacrifice for all
bugs and crawling life continuum.
Protector tree, supreme communicator
community leader, mother of all
tree. Sinewy branch, sturdy pine.
Tree that curves down my spine.
Fragrant and fatherly shade heaven.
Musty and musical, tree that forgives us
our trespasses. Tall and tempting tree that beckons
to climbers with two, four, six legs and more.
Tree I wear like a crown to soothe
my boggled mind and leave behind
my crumpled day.

Tree I desire. Tree of my insides.
Tree where I holler loud!

Now star-studded tree, magical maple syrup
tree of my dreams. I suck you, tree,
into my fragile heart while
walking in the woods.

I tree the earth.
Everything trees on this spinning orb
of constant reinvention.
Tree of animals, tree of oceans, tree of
mountains. Tree where my mind
belongs only to me.
Stronger than it seems tree. Gentler than
a feather breeze tree.
Tree who will be tickling the sky when you and I
are no more.

drift

the truth is you've got no roots to hold you steady

in this life of drifting, moving
starting over & over in another new place

you might toss & turn as you dream of people
you've known and wonder upon waking where

it could have possibly been now that you
find yourself in the southern mountains, where

you will never talk about or write about
grits or grandpa's fiddle or the front porch swing

you might float & break all kite strings as you drift left
or right over treetops to the east, lakes to the north where

your parents hailed from—couldn't wait to get away from
never knowing even at the age of sixty where

you might land where
you might feel at home.

Betty Makes a Five Layer Cake with a Blowtorch

Fingers in the fudge, butter knife held between her teeth, flame thrower gripped firmly, my artist friend attacks her baking the way she hurls herself at a blank canvas—all coiled energy and vision and a little violence thrown in for good measure—as the layers take shape but must be HOT to be frosted and her Louisiana skin is glowing, because that is all a southern belle is allowed, but the chocolatey cascading curls are definitely sweating profusely; later this creation will startle starving eyes and slide down newly betrothed gullets, along with their adoring onlookers who want to eat art.

How Do We

How do we number our days
tally our worries about loved ones
bemoan our troubled state
with any validity and weight
when the morning death toll—
each new fresh-kill dawn—
reports hundreds of children blindly
slaughtered in their sleep?

How do we comprehend the gore
and genocide across the ocean
laying waste to all other tragedies?

How do we pretend to have
a normal day, when lifting a glass
to our lips feels too privileged,
too decadent, when others have no
water at all?

Being so far away, how can we
make it any different?
Will our protests be heard
by the great capitalist war
machine?

How can we, ever again
return to our solitary
petty woes?

Rain (sex) Rain (sex) Rain

I want you on my face
Running rivers into my ears
Drowning my (fuck) muddled mind
Washing me clean

Transformed to a tall oak
Leaving me (raw) bark naked
Standing fertile
Timeless in my desire

Strip me to the core
Storm of nature's reproduction
Don't stop gushing
(Blow) me to and fro

Again, and again
I want more
Until I am soaked (wet) through
Laid prostrate with adoration

the dancer

purple light, red light, strobe light, black light, she walks on stage in tight white turned neon, wipes the pole long and lean with a wash rag, turns to talk to the DJ through the beaded curtain, slinks to the shaft and climbs it with ease in two shimmies, *(in my mind she's ten and climbing a thirty-foot flagpole)* flips upside down in a graceful gush of fluttering glitter, spins and spirals with butterfly arms reaching out, slides to the floor belly down like a slithering snake, but not before clicking her nine-inch sparkly heels—clack, clack—like an upside-down Dorothy wishing for home—then does a cat cow and a meow stretch before she twerks, tosses her blond ringlets, batting eyelashes—she's radiating ecstasy and we are riveted by her grace and pure comfort in the spotlight so bright, *(just yesterday I was running behind her bike without training wheels)* this complex artistry of removing garments while balancing on the platforms she commands with military precision, like a towering baby giraffe, all heads must look up to her dizzying height—she's the goddess of the underworld in the temple of the wayward lonely hearts, Jonesing for a lap dance, *(I remember how she got the jagged scar above her left knee)* and when the bra flies off Washingtons and Lincolns flutter down from the balcony like cherry blossom petals in the spring and she looks up and smiles demurely giving me a wink

MJM&me

after Oliver Baez Bendorf

And the way you used to. How perfectly oval your
fingernails pressed pink on the shower glass door.
The laughter ringing out of my throat when.
That giant sleigh bed where we would. Escaping.
Discovering the secrets of. Mad clawing.
No catching our breath. The stillness of your sleeping
head, eyes closed, mouth open. Our bodies pretzels.
Years ago. I still remember how. Desire I thought
was only for others. Whispers in the hallway
so as not to wake X and X.
        Now slower.
Now pillow talk some mornings.
         Love stretches.

Funeral Day

A morning so clear, I could fall in love
with everything
including myself. My family, you are the only ones
I surrender to without resignation.
The sky so pink. What's magic,
is magic. What's real
is us despite
a country so divided, so grieved, so troubled.
Our discontent loud as gunfire.
Listen. Even the mountains cry.
Put your ear to the earth, my love.
Let's breathe together.
What's death? What is death
becomes dawn.

How to Walk Your Dog

Begin by tossing your senile mom's prescription drugs down the toilet, then run through the house humming a tune until it hits you that they will all dissolve and end up in the city water system, or the ocean, worse, and pull your hair at your stupidity! When you hear her alarm go off, run to get the dog and whisper 'We have to get the hell outta here!' Dash to the car and sit still together while the engine warms. If you hear a whippoorwill, and feel the pink streaked sky cloud your mind, and the overhead light melts and drips into your coffee mug, then you are ready to be dragged through the woods by a fifteen-pound terrier who refuses to learn to fly (Don't boss him, don't cross him, he's wild in his anger)—No, wait, that was just the smell of stars crashing to the earth and the taste of your palms exploding in a joy you cannot explain for the beauty of this day. Don't worry, the rabbit can lead you home.

Sunday Ironing

a ritual like
so many we look
forward to. some
like crossword puzzles,
baking, or sewing—my
Zenlike practice entails
listening to Mozart
sometimes Chopin, then
the squeak and snap of
the ironing board cross-
ing its long legs, making
the dog cower— so
begins the meditation
iron turned to high linen
detangling a mass of
freshly washed one
hundred percent cotton
pillow cases, chaotic,
wrinkled, soon to be
flattened one by one
spraying a fine mist of
water— the sizzle so
satisfying as the burning
triangle presses them
envelope flat, the sweet
smell of hot linen rising
to my nose
fold in half **press**
fold in half **press**
making all the kinks
invisible if only I
could do the same
with my life
with the world,
folded, stacked and shelved

car wash orgasmic whirl

For only five dollars fed to the off-road robot, wheels lock into the wet shimmering drag system, neutral gears sucked into the bubbling bliss, leaving the world behind as me and my vehicle are mechanically pulled into a cave of cleansers and cacophony of motion. Seat tilted back to the maximum spaceman oblivion, radio rocks John Lee Hooker into my pelvis. Deep exhale as the water and light skate across my windshield dancing over my half-closed eyes; jaw-jiggling jelly roll for me and my old jalopy. Purple popping bubbles turn caterpillar green psychedelic liquid lava luminescence as giant rag eggbeaters pound the sides of my old gypsy wheels, shimmy shake me to shambles, expel us new and dripping, birthed into blinding brightness. Machine and mistress emerge cucumber clean, optimism in every turn. I call that a middle of the week miracle.

Ylva

(Swedish for she-wolf)

When I go home its always my daughters
who take me there.
We have no roots, no particular land or house
so it's always their voices, code words
of our secret language, that carry me.
The smell of their hair oil, their skin
like no other, that makes me feel
one of the pack.
No longer the alpha dog.
Not caring as long as I'm running
beside them, part of their
fears and failures. Their fierce howls
against the injustices of the world.
Their joys and successes in the hunt.

Listening to their whines, pants, yips
and the compassion they show
in slowing down for those at the rear—
sometimes limp footed me.
Proud that they came from me
but are their own wild selves
leading the way through this dark
mysterious wood, both new and familiar.
When moving in a pack, we are forever home.

my mother was a dancer

i am a dancer
my daughter is a dancer

we're genetically wired through our sinewy
muscles so the back beat just won't let us stop

moving memories of my mother clapping
twisting and turning
snapping her fingers, hips
gyrating in unknown patterns
feet skidding across
the kitchen floor
uncontrollable joy transported
to unknown pleasures
lost in the rhythm
eyes closed, lips parted
not my mom at all

here i am today
skating across the hardwood
of my tiny gallows kitchen
dipping and diving
shimmying and shaking
belting from the bottom
of my throat
heartbeat racing
jerking and jiving in my private
disco full well knowing

that my offspring
will be turning and twisting
in nine-inch heels, no less
mastering all the moves
down to a science
under the black lights

once there was hippy
chick called a free spirit
next an 80s girl
called a maniac on the dance floor
now a Gen Z exotic
dancer strutting her stuff

rhythm in our roots!

How to Drive Your Car

Start by waking up at 3 am because you are dreaming of your sister again, who isn't talking to you again, and make a cup of tea while you stare out the window at the dense black sky with no twinkle stars and your heart slips down like a wet sloppy sponge, sliding along your inner thigh until it hits your heel, so you can kick it and stomp it if you like but she'll still be mad at you because she hates the misery of her life, so you just reach down and grab it and slap it back in place then walk outside into the prickling cold with your slippers on to look at the sky and warm up the engine of your old Toyota (defroster purring like a cat) so you can drive down old country roads to nowhere until you can breathe again—No, wait, that was just the smell of all the frogs dying and the taste of man killing the planet and your tears crystalizing into diamonds as they scatter the mass grave. Don't worry, the elephants will still follow you home.

Saved

Not by Jesus, not by prayer, not by Satan's

underwear—just by science plain and simple

modern medicine to the rescue! Teased at school

for the enormous bunchy scar in the shape

of a T (for Terrific, mom said) in the middle of your tiny

chest, how could they have known the trauma at three

of a giant penicillin loaded needle jabbed

daily into your bruised butt cheek, how

you'd shriek, mom at your side through the long days,

hands grasping under plastic tent flaps for months.

They didn't see you marching down the hospital hallways

With a jar of coins on one hip, headed to the payphone

To call your dad, your rescuer, yelling loud and clear

"Come get me outta here!"

car conversation en route to the airport

she's curled into the front seat, feline, and looking intently into her phone, scrolling, texting and who knows what until we hit a bump and she looks up and I seize the moment to ask what her dad gave her for Christmas and she sighs and rolls her eyes and says *okay but this is just between us—both sis and I owe dad money so instead of a gift he just deducted money from our debt* and I want to scream but simply say *I guess you should feel lucky he's not charging you interest.* that's okay she says, *you make up for it by doing the holidays doubly big* and we both giggle—she looks out the window at the cold grey highway construction and the sluggish white nightmare sky where the sun can't break through the clouds and then I squeeze her leg, she squeezes my hand then winks at me, goes back to her phone, disappears into that void and I focus on the traffic, and we are somehow both smiling with bubbles floating out of our ears or maybe they are little pink hearts like the ones
                                she creates on her TikTok posts

late summer

all the delicate sinewy spiders
have left their egg sacks
in the corners of our porch
their valiant attempt
to carry out the lineage little
do they know the men
with pressure wash guns will
arrive next week and blast their
time-bomb creations with soapy
hot water into gutters and rails
a smashing crashing chemical death
which I just cannot stand
to think about this foggy morning
so I take the broom to the right
angles as gently as I can and wipe
their sacks so brown and round
fragile with hundreds of future
friends—into the yew shrubs,
their poisonous berries waiting to turn
my lips blue and stop my heart
in seconds but may just offer
hospitable shelter from the winter
winds and rain so that my
charming Charlottes can take
up residency next
spring on this old porch
to save me from the pesky flies
when we can all gaze out of our many
eyes at the hay field to watch
the deer and turkeys by turn
together.

vanish

wind in my face and we are all endangered
smell of night blooming jasmine, astronauts float as

we race down the dirty highways of extinction
sunlight filtered through green leaves on absent black rhinos

no longer in dreams and fiction foretold
ghosts of rustling book pages adored by their readers

the future is here, howling at our doors, claws of scorching heat
Sinu parakeet falls, islands sink, skyscrapers tumble like Jenga
   sticks

head bowed; I write you this letter on sheets of toilet paper
dying golden frogs, blue dotted gecko, best of all the silver birch

struck dumb as if I had lost my mother
in a blip of time on this spinning orb, all will vanish

Crashy

was my nickname. I'd fly from my crib as a toddler.
As soon as I could stand, I'd rock back and forth then hurl
myself forward—arms wide. I'd hit the floor and emit piercing
screams, much to my mother's dismay. She placed pillows around
the landing zone. Jumping from shopping carts to the cement
floors in supermarkets. Jumping from the top of the stairs.
Anything to feel the joy of flight, the momentary freedom.
Imagine my host's dismay the other night when dancing
I did a back flip over a chair and landed on my skull.
It was a dare, and I was showing off, but for a moment
I was flying, feet over head. Not exactly the expected
behavior for someone almost sixty. I felt a little bruised
and banged up the next morning, but there is nothing
like soaring through space to make you feel alive!

Listening

As I sat with her
and listened
hearing more than her words
seeing more than her tears
her nervous hands
her shifting body

I palmed her pain
I saw her searching eyes
I smelled her uncomfortableness
in her own skin
I tasted her sour disappointment

All I could do
was listen, finally
realizing that I had very little
to do with this, with her

even though
I birthed her

Her journey is her
own making, so what
is there to say
to someone you love so
deeply it hurts
would give your life for
except
to wish them self-love,
self-knowledge

So that is how we left it
mother and daughter
with those words, then
a hug that will hopefully help
down the road
(she drove away)

I just want you to
be happy (I said)
Love yourself

Fall Turning

after Patricia Fargnoli

If you have seen the leaves
twisting in the wind
colors of flame and fire landing in your hair
or somewhere slowly falling
into the glistening creek
to be carried downstream
then you have felt wonder
and know its longing.
And if you have crunched the leaves
only for the sound
of grinding beauty into dust,
for the continuum of the cycle,
particles in your nose and throat
like the molecules in the mysterious maple
the breeze stirring you
like the forlorn cry of a train whistle
then you can understand
how, more often than not,
death must precede life,
how only through ending
can we begin again,
this vibrant palette a last aria to summer
its fading shadows, the imprint
of leaf on cheek
as fleeting as childhood.
And this blaze of glory
as necessary as rolling down a grassy hill
laughter vibrating into earth
as urgent as that final kiss.

Wounded

The word wound sprang from injury
but also from grief.

The warrior Saxons spoke *wunda*
and *verwunden* as if it were a wonder

how such pain could happen, endure.
Now the word trauma is in fashion.

Shakespeare wrote "He jests at scars
that never felt a wound"

in 1596 on a cold winters' day while
the winds howled around his London *flet*

when words failed to sooth his fractured
heart over the dark lover who splashed

in his love's blood with boots of steel,
becoming Juliet to his Romeo.

My wound will not heal; neither
will my daughters—even when good memories

rain down in rivulets over my puzzled brain
to remind me again and again

no scab, no scar, will form
until I find some peace within.

Pointless to ask how long a wound can last
when we have no grasp of eternity.

Exalted

after Naomi Shihab Nye

The sugar cube is exalted by the ant.

The saucepan is exalted by the spatula.

The songbird is exalted by the silence
who waits with silken patience for the song to begin again.

The lasso is exalted by the cowboy
who is exalted by the horse, but only sometimes.

The sacrifice is exalted by the priest
when it doesn't haunt his dreams.

The knife is exalted by the hunter
who sometimes pays for his passion with his life.

The word, the right word, just the right word
is exalted by the writer.

I want to be exalted as a lover
of children playing pretend,
of having no fear of deep connection
or holding eye contact,
of smiling at strangers.

And maybe, just maybe,
after the burning of my cadaver,
living on in the memory
of the people I exalted.

empty

empty gut, empty hands, empty floors, empty halls, empty car, empty sky, dry empty throat—perhaps if i had been interested in birds when i was younger, more observant of their behavior, patterns, and lifestyle, i wouldn't be so slow to realize what a lasting heartbreak an empty nest can be, if i had really watched them but i dismissed them early on as petty, cruel, territorial, pecking, aggressive, selfish, pea brained; kicking their babes out of the nest on schedule, perhaps not even recognizing them next spring when their new eggs hatched, even though i know this is not the way of the swan and like most people on the planet now i have watched a handful of documentaries on heroic penguins facing harsh conditions, all those clownish tuxedo waddling birds holding the egg off the ice with their feet, just waiting for their mate to come throw up in their mouths and tag team parenting (how do they even know who is who in that sea of white and black?)—no, i cannot relate to birds at all because i have always been an elephant at heart, and i expected my two daughters to stay with my heard for at least twenty years or even their whole lives (elephants don't go off to college but even if they did i am sure they would return, right?) trapsing through the dust and mud or tall grasses in the brilliant African sun, eventually joined by their own babes, trunks entwined, spraying water, rolling in the ponds and frolicking in the rivers until the day i fell down dead, one autumn day after the long journey to the burial grounds, bleached bones in the graveyard, frequently visited and never forgotten—so why aren't i the wise-mother-leader, why is no one following me along the endless trail to the water hole because i know where it is and i miss their footfall, and i haven't forgotten, so don't talk to me about an empty nest and the necessity to fly off on your own, you feathered furies from hell, i'm still waiting for the return of my two babes, any day now, anytime they please, i'll be here waiting for my elephants to come home . . . but now it's time to put seed in the birdfeeders

Open Heart

(a poem to my younger self)

Was it because her chest was cracked as an
infant, ripped asunder & sewn up again

that she has always been wantonly willing
year after year to have her heart broken?

Doctors make no comment when asked if a
side effect of heart surgery could be

an addiction to breakage. Is it possible that
once cut, the pain of healing could feel like home?

How else to explain why she's always
trusting & diving deeply into love

with any quick—witted comedian
with a swagger, a smirk & one foot out the door?

Why else does she open the panes of her heart
out to the street like an Italian matron leaning

on the window ledge watching for young
lovers' bodies entwined in the noon heat?

Venire! she cries, already falling in love
with the afternoon sun on her cheek.

About the Author

Nicole Farmer has published two books of poetry, *Wet Underbelly Wind* (Finishing Line Press 2022) and *Honest Sonnets* (Kelsay Books 2023). Her poems have been published in *Wisconsin Review, Suisun Valley Review, Apricity, Wild Roof Journal, Poetry South, Drunk Monkeys, Sad Girls Club,* and many other journals. Nicole was awarded the first prize in prose poetry from *Bacopa Literary Review* in 2020. She lives in Asheville, North Carolina, with her husband and their stubborn Carin terrier.

Her website is:
NicoleFarmerpoetry.com